MY8

EMBRACE AND ENGAGE THE WONDER OF EVANGELISM

ED NEWTON

LifeWay Press®
Nashville, TN

ISBN: 9781430041467

Item number: P005737562

Dewey Decimal Classification Number: 248.83

Subject Heading: CHRISTIAN LIFE \ STUDENTS \ EVANGELISM

Printed in the United States of America

Student Ministry Publishing

LifeWay Church Resources

One LifeWay Plaza

Nashville, TN 37234-0144

We believe that the Bible has God for its author; salvation for its end; and truth, without any mixture of error, for its matter and that all Scripture is totally true and trustworthy. To review LifeWay's doctrinal guideline, please visit *www.lifeway.com/doctrinalguideline*.

TABLE OF
CONTENTS

ABOUT THE AUTHOR

Ed Newton was raised in a deaf world. The only child of two deaf parents, Ed was the voice in the silence for his parents, Ron and Libby Newton. Through difficult circumstances and major hardships, Ed was radically saved in high school. When he was a senior in high school, God used His Word and those of His followers to confirm Ed's call to ministry. God led Ed to Clearwater Christian College, where he had the opportunity to play college basketball for four years while getting a Christian education.

Ed continued his education journey, earning a Master in Religious Education from Mid-America Baptist Theological Seminary, a Master of Divinity from Trinity Theological Seminary, and a Doctorate of Ministry in Pulpit Communication and Expository Preaching from Trinity Theological Seminary.

Prior to surrendering to a call to an evangelism ministry, Ed has served the local church as a student minister, recreation minister, as well as serving as a minister of outreach and single adults. Currently, Ed serves in a support role as staff evangelist at First Baptist Church Central Florida, is the executive director of the LIFT TOUR, and a member of the teaching faculty at Student Leadership University in Orlando, Florida.

God has uniquely gifted Ed with an ability to connect with various age groups, both personally and corporately. His communication style can be summarized as "passion with content" while seeking to inspire people to be passionate, dedicated followers of Christ. He and his wife, Stephanie, and their four children—London, Lola, Liv, and Lawson—live in Orlando, Florida.

HOW TO USE

Welcome to **My 8**! This Bible study resource is designed to help you lead your students to understand both the heart and the how-to of evangelism.

This study for all students is designed to be used in a weekly small-group setting. However, feel free to follow a plan that meets the needs and schedule of your students.

WHAT YOU'LL NEED
- DVD player/TV or data projector
- Leader guide
- Student book for each student

This leader guide is designed to help you facilitate each group session. The group content is arranged into the following sections:

SESSION SYNOPSIS
A brief synopsis is provided at the beginning of each session to help you understand the theme and direction for this particular study at a glance.

WATCH
Each group session will begin by viewing the specific session video from the DVD. Each 7-9 minute DVD segment features the author, Ed Newton, providing a general overview that introduces and illustrates the session topic.

You'll find a viewer guide for students to use while watching the DVD at the beginning of each session in the student book. Encourage students to use the guide to follow the video and take notes on Ed's teaching. A completed viewer guide is provided in the leader guide.

Keep in mind that much of what is mentioned in the video will be covered in greater detail in the session study.

STARTING THOUGHTS
This section uses activities and/or discussion questions to introduce the biblical content.

CLOSER LOOK

This section contains the bulk of the biblical content. In this section—and also in "Starting Thoughts"—activity prompts and discussion questions will be marked in bold. Most of the activities and questions are found in the student book.

Space is provided in the student book for students to write their answers to the questions. However, feel free to use the questions as a way to prompt discussion.

NEXT STEPS

This section contains three elements:

- **Review**

  Students will be prompted to review the session and determine key points that made an impact on them.

- **My 8 List**

  In this section, students will record the names of unsaved people for whom they are praying. Students will be prompted to add a new name to the list after each session. At the end of the study, students will have a total of eight names on their lists.

- **Scripture Memory**

  Each week, students will be encouraged to memorize one passage of Scripture. All of these verses come from Romans, and most of them will be used in the gospel presentation discussed in Session 7. Students will have memorized eight verses at the completion of this study.

BONUS: MY 8 BRACELETS

Also available for purchase are **My 8** bracelets. These awareness bracelets consist of a three-fourth-inch metal 8, laid on its side, connected by an adjustable red band. The bracelet can serve as a constant reminder of the following things:

- the salvation each student has experienced;
- to pray for the eight people on their list;
- the eight verses they have memorized;
- the divine appointments God has designed for them.

The bracelet can also serve as a conversation starter with friends and strangers. Someone's curiosity about the bracelet could lead to an instant common-ground moment that quickly moves into a spiritual conversation.

We encourage you to purchase a bracelet for each student who completes the **My 8** study. These bracelets can be purchased at *lifeway.com/my8*.

SESSION 1 MY PICTURE

Session Synopsis

Session 1 introduces the direction of the study by briefly looking at the four main passages upon which the **My 8** journey is based. You will discuss in detail the first passage, Isaiah 8:1-8, helping students understand that grace motivates our witnessing, then highlight the other three passages.

WATCH

Watch the Session 1 video (included in the leader kit). Instruct students to follow along with the viewer guide on page 6 of the **My 8 Student Book.** *The answers are below.*

1. Evangelism is not just a request, it's a <u>COMMAND</u> from Scripture.

2. God could have chosen to spell out the gospel in the sky, but instead He has chosen to use <u>YOU</u> and <u>ME</u>.

3. The four key verses in the **My 8** strategy are:
   1. <u>Isaiah 6:8</u>
   2. <u>Matthew 28</u>
   3. <u>Acts 1:8</u>
   4. <u>Acts 8</u>

4. **Isaiah 6:8:** The calling on our lives to make Christ known is not <u>GUILT</u>, but <u>GRACE</u>.

5. **Matthew 28:** <u>WORSHIP</u> serves as the fuel for evangelism.

6. **Acts 1:8:** What (or Who) is the power source for evangelism? The <u>HOLY</u> <u>SPIRIT</u>

7. **Acts 8:** Acts 8 is a practical look at the <u>DIVINE</u> <u>APPOINTMENTS</u> God has given you to share the gospel.

Briefly review the key points of the video and allow time for discussion.

STARTING THOUGHTS

Lead students through this portion of the study, inviting group participation. Use the content after each question to enhance and direct the conversation.

Welcome students to the study, explaining that **My 8** is not a formula for sharing the gospel, but rather a lifestyle.

- **Are you able to see autostereograms? Do you even know what those are?**

Explain that autostereograms are 3-D pictures that on the surface just seem to be a series of colors and patterns. But if you stare at the picture long enough, you're supposed to be able to see an image behind the picture. Display examples from a Magic Eye® book or images printed from the Internet. Provide sufficient time for students to try to identify the hidden images, then discuss who could see the images and who couldn't.

- **Was this exercise enlightening or frustrating? Explain.**

Talk together about how frustrating it is when someone can see something that you can't. Direct attention back to the autostereograms and explain that the image isn't hidden; it's just that it's not evident, like the example Ed shared on the video about the FedEx® logo. Stress that when we're able to see something that's hidden, our instinct is to pass it on.

- **Have you ever had that experience? Explain. Be prepared to share a personal story.**

Direct attention to this paragraph in the My 8 Student Book and discuss:
"When you really see something, there's a high probability that you'll tell someone else about it. In a conversation with a friend or acquaintance, you'll probably find a way to share the insight you recently gained. There's a chance the person you're talking to may have already noticed whatever it is you've just come to understand. But what if that person reacts with enthusiasm and excitement because you've just shared information about something they've never understood? In all likelihood, the cycle will continue. The person you enlightened will enlighten someone else." *(My 8 Student Book, p. 7)*

- **How does this apply to us sharing the gospel?**

Explain that if we're not careful, we will assume that everyone around us is already a follower of Christ, or if not a follower, that they've heard the gospel and have declined it. However, this is not the case.

- **What's the danger in that kind of thinking?**

We must realize that there are people all around us—perhaps even some of our closest friends—who have not made a decision to follow Christ. Perhaps God is preparing their hearts to hear the good news again. He is wanting to collide our lives with theirs to bring about life transformation.

CLOSER LOOK

This section allows you and your students to dig deeper into the themes and topics Ed introduced in the video. Use the Scripture and information below to guide your discussion.

Write these four Scripture reference on a white board or large sheet of paper:
- *Isaiah 6:8*
- *Matthew 28:18-20*
- *Acts 1:8*
- *Acts 8*

- **What is the common factor in these references?**

Point out that the intent is not to be mystical or mysterious, or to say that the chapter and verse references were inspired by God. They are not. However, it is an interesting phenomenon that all these key passages have the number 8 in them. We will use this common factor to help frame our study: eight sessions, eight Scripture passages to memorize, eight names to pray for, and so forth.

Guide students to take a quick look at these four important passages which will guide and shape the rest of our **My 8** journey. Invite a student to read Isaiah 6:1-7 aloud, then allow students time to answer the following questions, also found on pages 8-9 of the student book . After a few minutes, discuss the questions together.

- **Who did Isaiah encounter in this passage? Why is that important?**

- **Describe the scene.**

- **Words and phrases are repeated in Scripture for emphasis. What words or phrases are repeated in this passage?**

- **Why are they significant? What do they teach you about God? About His glory and holiness?**

- **Look at verse 5. How did Isaiah respond to his encounter with the holy God? Why did he respond this way? Explain.**

Explain that when we see God for who He is and ourselves for who we are not, then we see the chasm of our sin and understand the utter hopelessness it creates.

Call for a volunteer to read Isaiah 6:7 aloud one more time.

- **How did God respond to Isaiah's confession? Explain.**

Point out that when Isaiah confessed his sin, the seraphim came with a burning coal, touched his mouth and made an incredible statement: "your wickedness is removed, and your sin is atoned for." Isaiah had done nothing to deserve the forgiveness he received. It was simply an act of mercy and grace of God.

You and I are in the same position. Like Isaiah, you and I stand guilty before a holy God, and there is nothing we can do through our own effort or power to make ourselves clean, righteous, or pleasing to Him. Yet God, in His great mercy and grace, sent Christ to be our sacrifice and our Redeemer. We did nothing to deserve this gift. Yet our sin, our shame, our guilt, is gone, all because of what Jesus did on the cross.

Direct students to write Isaiah 6:8 in the space provided in their student books (p. 9).

Use the questions below to discuss the passage.
- **What did God do after cleansing Isaiah from his sin?**

- **How did Isaiah's cleansing prepare him for God's call?**

- **What was Isaiah's response to God's call? How is this an appropriate response to God's work of salvation in our lives? Explain.**

Point out that Isaiah had no clue how this vision would end. All Isaiah knew was that his guilt had caused God's judgment to be unleashed. This prompted Isaiah's heart cry of "I am wrecked and ruined." But God acted according to His mercy and grace to forgive and cleanse Isaiah, who responded to God's call in obedience: "Here am I! Send me!" When we confess our sin and place our faith for salvation in Jesus, God's grace covers our sin and brings us from spiritual death to life. When you have experienced that transformation, there is only one appropriate response to God's call: *Here am I! Send me.* Move to the second key passage. Enlist a volunteer to read Matthew 28:18-20 aloud.

- **What do we call this passage? Why?**

This passage is called the Great Commission. It's where Jesus makes the future purpose of His followers very clear. Guide students to identify Jesus' commands in this verse. Challenge them to list the command in their own words in the space provided on page 10 of their student books. Point out that the call was to go and make disciples.

Read Matthew 28:17 aloud to help students learn more about the context of Jesus' call for His followers to make disciples.

Guide students to examine the passage in its entirety and help them to understand that those who received Jesus' mandate to "go into all the world" would do so in an attitude of worship. John Piper was spot-on in his book *Let the Nations Be Glad* when he wrote that worship fuels our evangelism.

Take a moment to recap what students have learned so far. Point out that Isaiah 6:8 shows us that when we experience God's grace and mercy, we respond in obedience. Matthew 28:17 helps us to understand that our obedience is fueled by worship and awe for the holy God who has saved us. Next, we move to Acts 1:8, which shows us the power source for carrying out the mission God has called us to.

Call on a student to read Acts 1:8. Direct students to write the verse in the space provided in their student books (p. 11).
  • **There are several key words and phrases in this passage, but what would you say is the first key word? Why did you pick that word?**

The word is *power.* This power guided Jesus throughout His ministry, led Him to the cross, then raised Him from the dead. This same power now lives in us. But we haven't been given this power to build our own kingdoms, but rather to expand the kingdom of God.

  • **How do we receive this power?**

Explain to students that the power we receive comes in the form of a person, the Holy Spirit. While the Spirit comes to live within us at salvation, we daily submit to His leadership. Without that submission, our efforts in evangelism will be futile. But if we allow the Holy Spirit to fill us and lead us, we will be empowered to accomplish the supernatural.

Point out that the last key passage of the **My 8** study, Acts 8, shows us some very practical, how-to tips for evangelism. Invite a student to read aloud Acts 8:26-39. Direct attention to page 11 of the student book and instruct students to summarize the passage in their own words in the space provided. After a few minutes, call for a few students to share their summaries.

Briefly emphasize how the divine collision between Philip and the Ethiopian official plays out. The Ethiopian official was reading a passage from Isaiah that points to Jesus' substitutionary sacrifice. Philip, led by the Holy Spirit, approached the Ethiopian man and asked a simple question. That question led to a conversation, which led to an opportunity for Philip to share Jesus with the Ethiopian man. Through the power of the Holy Spirit, a life was forever changed.

- **Do you think this kind of encounter can happen in your life? Explain.**

NEXT STEPS

Explain to students that at the conclusion of each **My 8** session, the "Next Steps" activities will lead them to reflect on what they've learned in each session. In addition, they'll also be challenged to pray for the unsaved people God has laid on their hearts and memorize Scripture that will prepare them to share their faith.

Review

Direct students to review Session 1 and the key verses. Challenge them to list some truths that stand out to them. After a few minutes, discuss some of the things the students listed.

My 8 List

Inform students that each week they will add a name to their **My 8 Lists.** Students will pray for the eight people they place on their list to come to know Christ. Today, encourage your students to record the name of the person who has been on their minds throughout this session. Invite the students to think about the people in their lives who are lost without Jesus—and write the name of the first person who came to mind on their **My 8 Lists.** Allow time for students to pray individually for the person whose name they listed.

Scripture Memory

Point out to your students that in order to share their faith, it helps to have an understanding of the biblical explanation of the gospel. This will help them understand the gospel and better equip them to explain it to those who need to hear the good news. State that the memory verse for this session is Romans 1:16:

> *For I am not ashamed of the gospel, because it is God's power for salvation to everyone who believes, first to the Jew, and also to the Greek.*

Close in prayer, thanking God for the students who have joined the **My 8** journey. Pray that you would all be bold witnesses for Him.

SESSION 2 **MY PROMISE**

Session Synopsis

Session 2 focuses on the second key passage in the **My 8** journey: Matthew 28:18-20. You will help students understand how important the promise of Jesus' constant presence is to carrying out the Great Commission. Students will also examine how evangelism and discipleship are both vitally important to the expansion of God's kingdom.

WATCH

*Watch the Session 2 video (included in the leader kit). Guide students to follow along with the viewer guide on page 14 of the **My 8 Student Book**. The answers are below.*

1. The four key passages of the **My 8** lifestyle are:
    1. <u>Isaiah 6:8</u>

    2. <u>Matthew 28</u>

    3. <u>Acts 1:8</u>

    4. <u>Acts 8</u>

2. What was Jesus' promise at the end of Matthew 28:20?
    <u>I WILL BE WITH YOU ALWAYS.</u>

3. What is the promise Ed makes to His wife?
    I am forever <u>FAITHFUL</u> to you.

4. Evangelism and discipleship are not compartmental <u>REALITIES</u>.

5. The reward of being obedient to the **My 8** journey is <u>JESUS</u>.

To debrief what students have just watched, briefly recap the key points of the video. Allow time for discussion or questions.

STARTING THOUGHTS

Lead students through this portion of the study, inviting group participation. Use the content after each question to enhance and direct the conversation.

Bring some pictures from your wedding or a friend's wedding. Pass the pictures around and allow the students to comment on the style of clothes, length of hair, and so forth. Share funny stories from your wedding or weddings you have attended. Allow students to also contribute stories. Talk about how weddings can have some humorous moments, but in essence it is a holy time in which those involved make serious promises. (*To make this more fun, gather wedding pictures from some of the students' parents and allow the students to guess whose parents are depicted in each photo. You could enhance this by using a PowerPoint® presentation.*)

Direct attention to page 15 of the **My 8 Student Book.** Challenge students to work individually or as a group to list some of the promises a bride and groom make at a wedding.

- **Do brides and grooms always keep those promises? Why or why not?**

- **What are some meaningful promises people have made to you in the past? Why were they so meaningful?**

- **Did those people keep those promises? Why or why not? Explain.**

Allow time for discussion, then point out that in the video and the student book, Ed talked about a promise he makes to his wife every time he leaves on a trip: *I am forever faithful to you.* Lead students to discuss what the promise means and why Ed makes it.

Point out that at the end of the Great Commission, Jesus made a promise that He will always keep: "And remember, I am with you always, to the end of the age" (Matt. 18:20).

- **Why is this promise so important to us as we carry out the Great Commission?**

Emphasize that Jesus wanted us to know that we are not alone as we carry the gospel to the ends of the earth, that He is faithful to us. Regardless of the circumstances or situations we face, Jesus is present to comfort, encourage, and guide us as we seek to share the hope of His gospel in a dark world.

CLOSER LOOK

This section allows you and your students to dig deeper into the themes and topics Ed introduced in the video. Use the Scripture and information below to guide your discussion.

- **What's the best pep talk you've ever gotten from a coach or leader? What made it so special? Why was it so encouraging?**

Point out that though a big pep talk from Jesus might have been fitting at the end of the Great Commission, Jesus didn't do that. Instead, Jesus chose to close His charge—and His earthly ministry—with a precious promise. Call for a student to read aloud Matthew 28:20, then direct students to write that verse in the space provided on page 16 of their student books.

- **Why was it important for Jesus to finish His charge to make disciples with a promise of His faithfulness?**

Explain that Jesus' promise helps us to understand two things: 1) As believers, we must walk in His constant presence; and 2) The first fruit of our reward for sharing the gospel is simply Jesus Himself.

To set this in context, enlist a volunteer to read Matthew 28:18-20 aloud to the group. Direct the students' attention to page 16 of their student books. Challenge them to list the key statements in the Great Commission in the space provided. Take a few minutes to review the students' lists.

Point out that in the Greek language, the word translated "go" in Matthew 28:19 is not an imperative command, but rather a present participle that means *as you are going*. Stress that the only command in the entire Great Commission is to "make disciples." Therefore, the key directive of the Great Commission is best rendered *since you are going, make disciples.*

Explain that sometimes in the local church, the Great Commission command to make disciples becomes all about discipleship. While there is a great need in the church for helping new and seasoned Christians grow in their faith, we can't afford to put all the emphasis there. Part of making disciples is sharing the gospel with the lost so that they can begin the journey of discipleship. With discipleship and evangelism, it's not either/or, but both/and.

- **Do you think your church puts more emphasis on discipleship or evangelism? What about your student ministry? Why?**

- **Is one supposed to be more important than the other? Explain your answer.**

Allow students time to discuss, then help them to understand that for discipleship to be effective it must be integrated into a strategy for evangelism. To think that evangelism and discipleship are two separate fronts is not the intent of the Great Commission. As Christians, we must live with an *as-you-are-going* mind-set, living life in the place where God has called us driven by one burning question:

- **Who is God putting in your path today who needs to hear the good news about Jesus?**

Challenge students to really think about that question. Direct attention to the scale on page 18 of the student book and instruct them to rate the importance level of that question in their daily lives. Allow students time to work, then call for a few volunteers to share how they rated the question and why.

- **If that truly was a burning question that was constantly on your mind, how would it change the way you live? Be specific.**

Point out that if that question was constantly on our minds, we would be much more aware of the opportunities all around us to share our faith. Sometimes, it seems that the only time that kind of radar is turned on in our hearts is when we are on a mission trip.

- **Why does it seem so much easier to share your faith on a mission trip than it does at home?**

Allow students to really wrestle with this question. Discuss how a mission trip causes us to be intentional with our lives. Because we're going somewhere with the intention of sharing the gospel, we have an expectation that God is going to do something extraordinary in and through us. We spend time and energy raising money, praying for the designated people group, taking cultural awareness classes, applying for passports, getting shots, sending out prayer cards, and gathering the supplies necessary for the trip. To put it simply, we spend a lot of time intentionally preparing and thinking about the mission trip and what we're going to do. All of these things are necessary to pull off a mission experience, and they all point us to the intentional effort of sharing our faith with the world.

- **Why don't see our lives as the constant mission trip?**

Explain that it seems like many believers have equated mission experiences with taking trips to designated locations rather than looking at where God has placed us—our homes, communities, schools, jobs, teams, and so forth—as the mission field.

- **In your church and student group, is there as big an emphasis on sharing your faith in your community as there is in sharing your faith on a mission trip? Explain your answer.**

- **Think about the mission experiences in your church. How do you measure the success on those trips?**

Help students understand that the primary reward for engaging in evangelism is not how many people we lead to salvation. Although that experience is so exciting and fulfilling, the reward for being on mission to share the gospel is simply Jesus. Guide students to see that when we are obedient to share our faith with someone, our reward is Jesus and the promise of His presence in the experience. Knowing that our obedience brings our Savior joy should also bring us deep satisfaction and great delight. Stress that His presence is enough. We don't need anything else to satisfy or motivate us. Just Jesus.

NEXT STEPS

Explain that we love to be rewarded for our effort. It's a tendency our culture encourages, inundating us with the idea that results equal rewards.

- **What are some examples of this mind-set you see in our culture?**

Allow students to share some examples, then point out how our culture often rewards results. Use examples from business, family, or school, such as how incentives are often used to motivate good grades. Stress that God calls us to a different kind of lifestyle. Believers shouldn't choose obedience to the Lord in order to receive a reward, but rather to experience the joy of living obediently for His glory as we rest in His promised presence.

Review
Direct students to review Session 2 and list some truths that stand out to them. After a few minutes, discuss some of the things they listed. Use the content on page 20 of the student book to guide you.

My 8 List
Direct students to fill in the first slot on their lists with the name of the person they added last week. Challenge them to think about the people God has placed in their lives, specifically someone who has a lot of influence but isn't a believer. God could work through this person's life to make a huge impact if he or she became a Christian. Instruct students to write that person's name in the second place on their lists. Provide time for students to pray silently for that person, asking that God would cultivate a deep burden to share Jesus with him or her.

Scripture Memory
Explain that an important part of memorizing is reviewing what you've already committed to memory so that you don't forget it. Challenge students to recite last week's memory verse, Romans 1:16.

This week, add Romans 3:10 to the list of verses your students are memorizing:
> . . . as it is written: There is no one righteous, not even one.

End the session with prayer. Lead the students to gather with a partner or a small group to pray for each other and the people whose names they have recorded on their lists.

SESSION 3 MY PROBLEM

Session Synopsis

Session 3 centers on the fears that can paralyze us when it comes to living out our faith and sharing the gospel. In this session, you'll guide students to examine their legitimate concerns about sharing their faith. Students will come to understand that Jesus offers true peace that equips us to live in bold confidence that only He can provide.

WATCH

Watch the Session 3 video (included in the leader kit). Guide students to follow along with the viewer guide on page 22 of the **My 8 Student Book.** *The answers are below.*

1. Like the early church, we are crippled by <u>FEAR.</u>

2. Why is Christianity thriving in places like Africa, Central and South America?
   <u>POVERTY</u> and <u>PERSECUTION.</u>

3. When you have nothing, Jesus is <u>EVERYTHING</u>.

4. We are resource <u>RICH</u>, but commitment <u>POOR</u>.

5. We have the greatest privilege in all the earth: to carry the name of <u>JESUS</u>.

6. The gospel is in places where we have so many resources, and the answer to the problem is unleashing those resources. How are those resources unleashed? By you being <u>OBEDIENT</u> to what God has called you to do.

Briefly review the key points of the video and allow time for discussion.

STARTING THOUGHTS

Lead students through this portion of the study, inviting group participation. Use the content after each question to enhance and direct the conversation.

Direct attention to the list of brands on page 23 in the student book. Explain that the list contains what *Forbes* magazine[1] considers the world's most valuable brands, but the brands aren't listed in the correct order. Direct students to arrange the brands in top 10 order. This activity can be completed individually or as a group. Allow students time to work, then reveal the correct order, printed below.

1. Apple®
2. Microsoft®
3. Google®
4. Coca-Cola®
5. IBM®
6. McDonald's®
7. General Electric Company®
8. Samsung®
9. Toyota®
10. Louis Vuitton®

Debrief with the following questions:
- **Why do you think these brands are listed as the most valuable?**

- **Why are these brands so well-known?**

- **Do you think the names of these brands are more well-known than the name of Jesus? Why or why not?**

Review what Ed said in the video about Coke. Point out that the Coca-Cola Company has been in existence for around 125 years, and, according to research, more than 94 percent of the world has heard of this product. Point out that a soda company has been more efficient in making their product known than Christians have been in making Jesus known in the world. And we had an estimated head start of 1,875 years! Help students understand the gravity of that statement by informing them that 3 billion people have never heard about Jesus. Explain that there are 5,924 people groups on the planet that have little or no access to the gospel.

- **So most of them have heard of Coke, but they have no clue who Jesus is. Why should that be a wake-up call to us to carry the name of Jesus unashamedly to the world?**

CLOSER LOOK

This section allows you and your students to dig deeper into the themes and topics Ed introduced in the video. Use the Scripture and information below to guide your discussion.

Remind students of the quote Ed once heard from a missionary and discussed in both the video and the student book: *"The church of Jesus Christ in America is resource-rich, but commitment-poor."*

- **How would you explain the statement in your own words?**

- **Do you agree with it? Why or why not?**

- **What might be some reasons our commitment to be on mission for Christ is poor?**

Direct students' attention to the early followers of Jesus. Point out how they struggled to move out and share the story. Call on a student to read aloud John 20:19,26.

- **What phrase appears in both of these verses?**

- **What emotion was dictating the actions of these followers? Explain.**

Point out that John 20 reveals the disciples were gathered in secrecy behind a locked door, afraid for their lives. Fear had paralyzed them all, causing them to look inward instead of outward. But Jesus addressed their fear. Invite a student to read aloud the entire passage, John 20:19-26.

- **What did Jesus repeatedly say to His followers in these verses?**

Share that Jesus responded to His followers' fear with one beautiful phrase: "Peace be with you." Stress that this same peace is at the core of the gospel we're called to share.

Direct students to read and summarize the following passages of Scripture:
- **Romans 5:1**
- **Ephesians 2:11-15**
- **Colossians 1:19-20**

Explain that Scripture makes it clear that when someone comes to a saving knowledge of Jesus Christ, that person is transferred from being an enemy of God (Col. 1:29-20; Eph. 2:11-15) to having peace with God (Rom. 5:1). Explain that this idea of peace goes deeper than a general sense of tranquility. The picture here is of the peace that comes when a war is ended. Hostilities have ceased and those who were once enemies have been reconciled. The war is over, and we can have a relationship with God. Guide students to understand that we who have peace with God should share with others how to have that same kind of peace. Emphasize that the peace we experience in salvation is the same peace that allows us to share the gospel with no fear. Stress that Jesus' peace equips His followers to operate in an unspoken confidence that only He can provide.

- **Unfortunately, some people look elsewhere for peace. What are some things you see your non-Christian friends are trusting to provide a sense of peace in their lives?**

Discuss how students and adults attempt to fill the longing or emptiness in their hearts with the things of the world—fame, money, power, possessions, relationships, popularity, and so forth. For some it can be all-consuming. Discuss how our culture is willing to spend thousands of dollars to obtain the things we think will bring us peace and contentment, when real peace is priceless. It cannot be bought or earned, nor can it be found in anything of this world. Only Jesus gives the peace that fulfills our longing.

- **What does it mean to say that Jesus is your peace? Explain.**

- **How have you experienced the peace of Christ through salvation?**

- **How have you experienced Jesus' peace as you continue to walk with Him?**

Talk with students about how even though Jesus brings peace to us through salvation, there are times we still struggle with fear. Stress that fear seems to be at the top of the Enemy's list of ways to attack God's people and keep them from being effective, especially when it comes to sharing our faith.

Help students to better understand this by directing their attention to the list of statements on page 27 of the student book. Challenge students to circle all of the statements that describe their hesitancy to witness to those who don't know Jesus:

- **I don't know what to say.**
- **I don't know how to begin the conversation.**
- **He might get defensive.**
- **She may never talk to me again.**
- **Our friendship will never be the same.**
- **I might not have the answers to their questions.**
- **I will no longer fit in with my closest friends.**

- **What else would you add to the list? Why?**

Stress that many of the things on that list are legitimate concerns about what could happen if we intentionally share Jesus with others. Agree with students that their relationships might change if they shared the gospel with a friend. It's entirely possible that your students—or you!—could struggle to know how to answer someone's questions. People may reject us when we share our faith. Point out, though, that if we focus on the negative possibilities, we'll be paralyzed by fear and never share our faith.

- **What if the opposite is true of everything you circled?**

Push students to consider that the opposite of all their fears could be true—that when they approach someone and share Jesus with him or her, that person's heart could be open to the gospel and the person could receive Christ!

- **If that possibility were to happen, wouldn't it be worth conquering your fears to see life change take place?**

Challenge students that they will never know if they never choose to push past their fear and rest in the peace of Jesus.

SOURCES

[1] "The World's Most Valuable Brands." *Forbes*. November 1, 2014. Accessed December 16, 2014. *http://www.forbes.com/powerful-brands/list/.*

NEXT STEPS

Explain to students that honestly evaluating why they are afraid to share their faith is a vital step in embracing and engaging the wonder of evangelism. Remind students that we often find it much easier to share the gospel with people we don't know rather than those we know quite well because we fear rejection or ridicule from someone we love. Stress that in the midst of all that, we must remember that it's not our job to save anyone; only God can do that. We must be obedient to share the gospel, trusting in Jesus' peace and presence as we do so, and leave the rest to Him.

REVIEW

Guide students to review the session and list some key truths that stand out to them. After a few minutes, discuss some of the things your students listed.

My 8 List

Direct students to add the first two people they are praying for to their **My 8 List** on page 28 in the student book. Direct them to write the name of the person they are most frightened to share their faith with on the third line. This should be someone the student might be concerned about being rejected by—an authority figure, friend, or even a family member. Invite students to confess their fear to God and pray that He would give them the courage to share the gospel with that person and provide an opportunity to do so.

Scripture Memory

Review Romans 1:16 and 3:10 as a group. Direct students to add Romans 3:23 to the verses they are memorizing:

> *For all have sinned and fall short of the glory of God.*
> *—Romans 3:23*

Close the session by providing a time for students to confess their fears to the Lord, thank Him for His peace, and pray that He would give them courage to share the gospel with boldness.

SESSION 4 **MY POWER**

Session Synopsis

This session focuses on the Holy Spirit. Students will come to understand that they aren't called to share the gospel in their own strength, but rather through the Holy Spirit's power. You will examine Acts 2 to see how the Holy Spirit worked within the lives of believers in the early church, empowering them to be bold for Jesus in difficult circumstances.

WATCH

Watch the Session 4 video (included in the leader kit). Guide students to follow along with the viewer guide on page 30 of the **My 8 Student Book.** *The answers are below.*

1. When you call upon the name of the Lord to be saved, your body becomes the <u>TEMPLE</u> of the living God.

2. The role of the Holy Spirit within you is not only to clarify Scripture, convict us of sin, but also to <u>CONFORM</u> us to the image of Jesus Christ.

3. When does the Holy Spirit come upon us? In that moment of <u>SALVATION</u>.
   And what does He do in and through us?
   He mobilizes us to be the <u>HANDS</u> and <u>FEET</u> of Jesus.

4. As you submit and surrender to the plan and purpose of God, realize that the Holy Spirit is actively at <u>WORK</u> within you each and every day.

5. What gives you the boldness to speak the name of Jesus?
   The <u>HOLY SPIRIT</u> within you.

Briefly recap the key points of the video. Allow time for discussion or questions.

STARTING THOUGHTS

Lead students through this portion of the study, inviting group participation. Use the content after each question to enhance and direct the conversation.

Direct students to list as many names of people they know as possible in one minute in the space provided on page 31 of the **My 8 Student Book.** After the minute, award a small prize to the student with the longest list.

Next, direct students to list all the places they've been in the last week in the space provided on page 31 in the student book. Provide the same time limit and award a small prize to the student with the longest list of places.

Point out that students know lots of people—family members, classmates, teammates, friends in band, chorus, theater, clubs, and so forth. Guide them to look over their lists of places and note that they go lots of places—to the gym, the store, the library, their jobs, the bank, the locker room, home, school, and so forth. Stress that in each of these places, students come face-to-face with more people, many of which not on their lists. Challenge students with this sentence: *All of those people and every one of those places represent multiple opportunities to share your faith.*

Explain that every day we have opportunities to—not obligations!—to share the hope we have in Jesus with others. We should want every person that God puts into our paths to come to know Him personally.

- **Does that feel a little overwhelming? Why or why not?**

Explain that when we look at our lists and see all of those names and places and think about sharing the gospel with each one, it does feel impossible. Even sharing with a few of them seems overwhelming, because it is—in our own power. Stress that God has not called us to share the gospel in our own power. Explain that He doesn't send us out equipped only with our meager courage, faltering words, and timid personalities. Instead, God Himself empowers us to share the gospel. And with Him, nothing is impossible (Matt. 19:26).

CLOSER LOOK

This section allows you and your students to dig deeper into the themes and topics Ed introduced in the video. Use the Scripture and information below to guide your discussion.

Lead students in a short review of Session 3. In order to do so, enlist a volunteer to read aloud John 20:19-22.

- **What was the emotional state of the disciples? Why?**

- **How did Jesus approach them? Explain.**

Remind students that fear was paralyzing the disciples. They were trembling behind a locked door, but then Jesus stepped in with His pronouncement: "Peace to you!" Explain that the Scripture you and the students studied in Session 3 helped you to understand that Jesus has brought peace to all of us through His finished work on the cross. Explain that because we have peace with God through salvation, we are now enabled to help others experience that peace by sharing the gospel with them.

Emphasize to students that we don't do that in our own strength or power. The Holy Spirit empowers us to share the gospel.

- **What comes to mind when you consider the Holy Spirit?**

Invite students to discuss that question. You may want to use the space provided on page 32 of the student book to help students to outline or even sketch their ideas. Point out that in many churches, perhaps even yours, the Holy Spirit isn't talked about much.

Draw attention to the quotation from Francis Chan's book *The Forgotten God* on page 32 of the student book. Chan stated that in most churches, the Holy Spirit is "mostly a forgotten member of the Godhead whom we occasionally give a nod of recognition to." He went on to say that most Christians "don't think we need the Holy Spirit. We don't expect the Holy Spirit to act. Or if we do, our expectations are often misguided or self-serving. Given our talent set, experience, and education, many of us are fairly capable of living rather successfully (according to the world's standards) without any strength from the Holy Spirit."[1]

- **Do you agree with Francis Chan's assessment? Why or why not?**

Explain that without the presence of the Holy Spirit at work in the heart of the believer, anything we try to accomplish for God will be futile. In fact, it will mostly be filled with fear and frustration.

Invite a student to read John 20:21-22 aloud. Point out that Jesus knew His followers needed His constant presence and power, so He did something for them they could not do for themselves when He visited the upper room. Explain that in this moment when Jesus spoke of the Holy Spirit, He was pointing them to the promise He would make right before His ascension.

Call for a student to read that promise in Acts 1:8.

- **What was Jesus' promise in this passage?**

- **When did that promise come to pass?**

Direct a student to read aloud Acts 2:1-4, and explain that the promised Holy Spirit arrived and filled the early believers, empowering them at that very moment to share the gospel in the languages of all the people who had gathered in Jerusalem. The Holy Spirit then further empowered them to take the gospel to the uttermost parts of the earth.

Point out the passages in Acts listed on pages 33-34 of the **My 8 Student Book.** Challenge students to look up the passages and record how the Holy Spirit worked through the first believers. Students can work individually or you may want to group them into pairs or small teams. Allow students time to work, then invite them to share their findings. Use the information below to help students understand why each passage was included.

- **Acts 2:4**
  The apostles were able to speak in different languages so that the Jews who were from other nations heard them speaking "the magnificent acts of God" (Acts 2:11) in their own languages.

- **Acts 4:31**
  They spoke God's message with boldness.

- **Acts 8:29**
  The Holy Spirit guided Philip to encounter and share the gospel with an Ethiopian official on his way home from Jerusalem.

- **Acts 13:2**
  Barnabas and Paul were set apart for mission work by the Spirit's prompting.

- **Acts 13:6-10**

  Filled with the Holy Spirit, Paul confronted a sorcerer on the island of Cypress.

- **Acts 16:6-7**

  The Holy Spirit prevented Paul and his companions from speaking the message in Asia.

- **Acts 20:23**

  Paul said that the Holy Spirit had revealed to him what was in his future.

Help students understand that this same Holy Spirit—the One who raised Jesus from the dead, came with power on Pentecost, filled the first believers, and led them to accomplish great things for the kingdom—is the same Spirit who lives in them.

- **Do you really believe that is true? Why or why not?**

- **If so, how have you seen the Holy Spirit work powerfully in and through a believer's life, whether you or someone else?**

Invite a student to read Ephesians 1:11-14. Let your students know that these verses will help explain when believers receive the Holy Spirit.

- **When does Paul say we receive the Holy Spirit?**

Explain that at the moment of salvation, the Holy Spirit comes to live within the life of each believer. (If students need more explanation, point them to the paragraph at the top of page 35 in the student book.) Point out that through the Holy Spirit, believers operate within the very same power that navigated Jesus during His earthly ministry. Help students understand that just as Jesus promised, the Holy Spirit lives in believers to comfort us (John 14:16), convict us (John 16:8), teach us (John 14:26), lead us (Rom. 8:12-16), and empower us (Acts 1:8).

Emphasize to students that as we walk in submission to the Holy Spirit, we will accomplish great things in His power for the kingdom of God. It is the Holy Spirit who empowers us to walk in obedience to the Lord. It is the Holy Spirit who empowers us to flee from sin. And it is the Holy Spirit who empowers us to share the gospel.

SOURCES
[1] Francis Chan, *Forgotten God*, (Colorado Springs, CO: David C. Cook 2009), 31.

NEXT STEPS

Explain to students that it's easy for us to forget the Holy Spirit is living in us. Encourage them to make it a habit to surrender to the Spirit's leading each morning, then intentionally turn their hearts to hear Him. Talk with them about cultivating a constant God-consciousness, meaning that in every segment of every day, they make an intentional effort to "pray continually" (1 Thess. 5:17).

Talk with students about practical ways they can intentionally create God-consciousness in their lives, particularly through the use of reminders that continually point them to the Spirit's work in their lives. Discuss the reminders Ed mentioned on page 36 of the student book, such as:

- A glow-in-the-dark bracelet that reminds Ed to shine the light of Jesus in the darkest places.
- How washing his hands reminds Ed of God's cleansing over his life.
- How glancing at his wedding band reminds Ed to pray for his family.

Explain that these reminders might not work for you, but encourage and challenge students to create reminders of their own that help them live surrendered to the leading of the Holy Spirit each day.

Review

Lead students to review the session and list some truths that stand out to them. After a few minutes, discuss some of the things the students listed.

My 8 List

Instruct students to write the first three names from their previous list on this week's list. Then, lead them to pray for these three people, praying each person on their lists would come to the place in their own journey where nothing would satisfy them. Pray that God would draw them to Himself as the only one who can satisfy.

Direct them to ask the Holy Spirit to place the fourth name on their list. Ask Him to lay on their hearts the name of someone who needs to hear the gospel. Also ask Him to confirm it and clarify it over the next few days. Challenge students to record this name on their list.

Scripture Memory

Instruct students to add Romans 5:8 to their list of **My 8** memory verses. Then, close the session by directing them to choose a partner and go over the first three memory verses: Romans 1:16; Romans 3:10; and Romans 3:23.

> *But God demonstrates his own love for us in this: While we were still sinners, Christ died for us.* —Romans 5:8

SESSION 5 MY PERSECUTION

Session Synopsis

In this session, you'll discuss the reality of persecution for believers. Students will be reminded that Jesus told His followers to expect persecution. You'll also investigate how persecution fueled the growth of the early church. Students will be challenged to wrestle with their own attitudes toward persecution and how to respond when it happens.

WATCH

Watch the Session 5 video (included in the leader Kit). Guide students to follow along with the viewer guide on page 38 of the **My 8 Student Book.** *The answers are below.*

1. Peter, under great scrutiny, said "We cannot help but to speak of the things in which we have <u>SEEN</u> and <u>HEARD</u>."

2. Following Jesus is <u>COSTLY</u>. Speaking up for Jesus may mean you might be <u>MISUNDERSTOOD</u>. But you cannot take that as a <u>CRITICISM</u>. You have to take that as a <u>COMPLIMENT.</u>

3. In Acts 5:41, the early disciples considered it a great <u>HONOR</u> to be dishonored for the sake of Jesus.

4. When you stand up for Jesus, you never stand <u>ALONE</u>.

5. Persecution actually is the means and mechanism by which the gospel goes forward in great <u>ADVANCEMENT</u>.

6. When persecution comes for us, may we, like the early disciples, say the same thing, "I consider it a great <u>HONOR</u> to face dishonor for the sake of Jesus."

Discuss with students the key points of the video. Allow time for any questions.

Lead students through this portion of the study, inviting group participation. Use the content after each question to enhance and direct the conversation.

- **Have you ever felt mistreated? Explain.**
  (If your students need further preparation before sharing their answers, use the activity and space provided on page 39 of the student book to help them gather their thoughts.)

- **Most of us know what if feels like to be treated unfairly or cruelly. But has that ever happened because you were a Christian? Has anyone ever physically or verbally attacked you because you claim the name of Jesus? If so, when? If not, why not?**

Discuss the following statistics (also found on page 39 of the **My 8 Student Book**) with students:

- Christians are the most persecuted religious group worldwide. An average of at least 180 Christians around the world are killed each month for their faith.[1]
- Christians in more than 60 countries face persecution from their governments or surrounding neighbors simply because of their belief in Christ.[2]
- One of the worst countries in the world for the persecution of Christians is North Korea. With the exception of four official state-controlled churches in Pyongyang, Christians in North Korea face the risk of detention in the prison camps, severe torture and, in some cases, execution for practicing their religious beliefs. North Koreans suspected of having contact with South Korean or other foreign missionaries in China, and those caught in possession of a Bible, have been known to be executed.[3]
- In 41 of the 50 worst nations for persecution, Christians are being persecuted by Islamic extremists.[4]

- **What are your thoughts when you hear these statistics?**

- **Why shouldn't these statistics surprise you? Explain.**

Call on a student to read aloud John 15:18-21.

- **What did Jesus say His followers could expect?**

- **Why did Jesus say believers would be treated this way? Explain.**

Point out that Jesus made it clear that if we follow Him, we will experience persecution.

- **Why do we as modern believers sometimes believe that we won't face opposition in sharing the gospel?**

If we follow Christ we will be opposed. Point out that when someone comes to saving faith in Christ, that person experiences a change in citizenship, from the kingdom of the world to the kingdom of heaven. That is something that Satan doesn't want to happen! Explain that the fact that we do face persecution from a world that wants nothing to do with our Jesus is actually confirmation that what we are called to be is real and legitimate.

CLOSER LOOK

This section allows you and your students to dig deeper into the themes and topics Ed introduced in the video. Use the Scripture and information below to guide your discussion.

Explain that in our humanity, we might fear persecution or view it as a terrible thing. Stress that even though we might feel that way, throughout history, persecution has served as one of the primary agents for the advancement of the gospel. As early church father Tertullian said, "The blood of martyrs is the seed of the church."

- **How do you think persecution advances the gospel?**

To help students grasp this concept, lead them through a short study of the early church. Enlist a volunteer to read Acts 2:42-47 aloud.

- **What words would you use to describe the early church? Why?**

- **What do these verses reveal about how the surrounding community responded to the early church? Explain.**

State that the early church enjoyed favor with the community for a short period of time. But that quickly changed. Direct students to read Acts 3:1–4:3 silently. Invite them to summarize the key points of the passage in the space provided on page 40 of their student books. Allow students time to work, then call for a few volunteers to share their findings.

Point out that after Peter and John healed the lame man, Peter began to preach the gospel. His words annoyed the religious leaders who had Peter and John arrested. Direct the students' attention to Acts 4:4. Point out that even in the midst of persecution, the church was growing.

Group students into teams and direct each team to prepare a marketing message for their church that centers on the role of persecution in evangelism. For example, a marketing tagline might be: *Hey, join us here and grow the church! All it takes is just a few nights in prison and some beatings.* Provide time for teams to work, then allow each group to share their ideas.

- **Do you think many people would sign up for this? Why or why not?**

- **If you had been Peter or John in this situation, how would you have responded to your persecutors? Why?**

Instruct students to read Acts 4:5-20 silently, then direct them to summarize how Peter and John actually responded to their persecutors in the space provided on page 41 of the student book. Call for a few volunteers to share their work.

Focus students' attention on Acts 4:19-20. Emphasize that Peter and John made it clear that nothing would keep them from speaking about what they had seen and heard.

Recruit a student to read Acts 4:23-31 aloud, then discuss how the early church responded to this event. Point out that they didn't pray for God to rescue them from the persecution, but instead prayed for more boldness to proclaim the message of Christ!

- **Do you think your church would respond in that manner? Why or why not?**

Inform students that the persecution of the early church only grew worse after this point in history. Enlist a volunteer to read aloud Acts 5:27-28 to discover the reason why. Explain that the apostles and the early church were determined to share about Jesus no matter what they faced.

Direct students to think about how they would respond if officials with guns burst into the room right now and ordered us to stop meeting and quit talking about Jesus, even threatening to imprison and beat us if we continued. Point out the list of possible reactions (printed on the next page and on page 42 of the **My 8 Student Book**). Challenge students to complete the activity, then discuss their answers.

What do you think you would do? Circle the answers you think best fit your response.

- *I'd think God had abandoned us.*
- *I'd be scared for my life.*
- *I'd deny that I was part of the group.*
- *I'd be mad at God for allowing this to take place.*
- *I'd never go back to the study.*
- *I'd be bold and continue to declare Jesus' name.*
- *I'd have to think long and hard about what to do next.*
- *Other: _____*

Call on a volunteer to read Acts 5:29,41-42 and discuss how the early church responded to the persecution they were facing. Emphasize that the early church continued to minister and teach because they were motivated by obedience. Point out that this motivation emboldened Stephen in Acts 7. Using God's long history with the Jews as his starting point, Stephen boldly proclaimed the gospel to the religious leaders of the day, using Old Testament Scriptures they would have been deeply familiar with. Summarize Stephen's message, then call for a student to read aloud Acts 7:54-60.

- **What stands out to you in this account? Why?**

Be sure to point out Acts 7:55-56, where Stephen sees Jesus standing at the right hand of God. This is significant because in other passages, Jesus is referred to as being seated upon His throne. But in this moment, Jesus is described as standing. While scholars differ about the significance of this uncharacteristic position, many understand it as Jesus rising to welcome the first Christian martyr in honor.

- **What were Stephen's last words?**

- **Where did he receive such inspiration?**

Point out that Jesus spoke similar words to his captors from the cross, when He asked God to forgive His executioners because "they know not what they do" (Luke 23:34).

Invite a student to read aloud Acts 8:1, then point to the paradox of this moment. Saul, believing he was acting for God, was condemning a man to death, and Jesus, the Son of God, was standing in approval of that man's willingness to die so that others would come to know Him.

- **How does this moment begin to fulfill what Jesus proclaimed in Acts 1:8? Explain.**

Explain that this moment begins the fulfillment of the church taking the gospel to the ends of the earth. Saul, who became Paul, would be responsible for spreading the gospel to the Gentiles. Because of his witness, the church would expand beyond Jerusalem, Judea, Samaria, and to the ends of the earth, fulfilling what Jesus proclaimed in Acts 1:8.

NEXT STEPS

Encourage students that while it may seem they are alone standing for Jesus, they are not. They have brothers and sisters in Christ all over the globe standing with them. Remind them that their willingness to live in obedience to God and proclaim Christ in the face of persecution will continue the global expansion of the gospel Jesus set in motion in Acts 1:8.

Review

Invite students to mull over all they've learned about the early church and the reality of persecution in this session. Challenge them to think about how God used His Word to bring them to new understanding or change the way they think or live. Direct them to jot down three key points they learned from this session on page 44 of their students book. Allow time for a short discussion of their responses.

My 8 List

Direct students to pray by name for the first four people on their **My 8 Lists** found on page 44 of their student books. Then, challenge them to add a fifth name: the person in their lives who they think is least likely to become a Christian. Urge them to consider the ramifications to their school and community if this person were to become a follower of Christ. Provide time for students to pray. Encourage them to pray that God would remove the spiritual blinders from the people whose names they recorded, allowing them to see their desperate need for Jesus.

Scripture Memory

Direct students to review the following memory verses: Romans 1:16; Romans 3:10; Romans 3:23; and Romans 5:8.

Challenge them to add Romans 10:9 to the list this week:

If you confess with your mouth, "Jesus is Lord," and believe in your heart that God raised Him from the dead, you will be saved.

SOURCES

[1] "5 Facts About Christian Persecution." Accessed December 16, 2014. *http://erlc.com/ article/5-facts-about-christian-persecution.*

[2] *Ibid.*

[3] *Ibid.*

[4] *Ibid.*

SESSION 6 MY PREPARATION

Session Synopsis

In this session, you'll learn that being prepared to share the gospel simply means being prepared to be obedient to the Holy Spirit. Students will dive into Acts 8, studying Philip's obedience to the Holy Spirit's call and how God used that obedience to lead Philip to a divine collision. Both Sessions 6 and 7 deal with aspects of Philip's interaction with the Ethiopian man. Look ahead so that you understand the difference between the two sessions.

WATCH

Watch the Session 6 video (included in the leader kit). Guide students to follow along with the viewer guide on page 46 of the **My 8 Student Book.** *The answers are below.*

1. In Acts 6, Philip is spoken of as being full of <u>WISDOM</u> and full of the <u>HOLY SPIRIT</u>.

2. Philip had the same <u>MEASUREMENT</u> of the Holy Spirit within him as you and I have within us.

3. When the Spirit begins to help us be mobilized for the sake of the gospel, we have to respond in <u>OBEDIENCE.</u>

4. It's not about ability, it's about <u>AVAILABILITY</u>. And the true mark of being a Christ-follower is saying <u>YES</u> to the command when He speaks into ours souls.

5. In John 14:15, Jesus said "If you love me, you'll keep my <u>COMMANDS.</u>"

To debrief what students have just watched, briefly recap the key points of the video. Allow time for discussion or questions.

STARTING THOUGHTS

Lead students through this portion of the study, inviting group participation. Use the content after each question to enhance and direct the conversation.

Direct students to complete the activity measuring their obedience on page 47 of the student book. Discuss their responses.

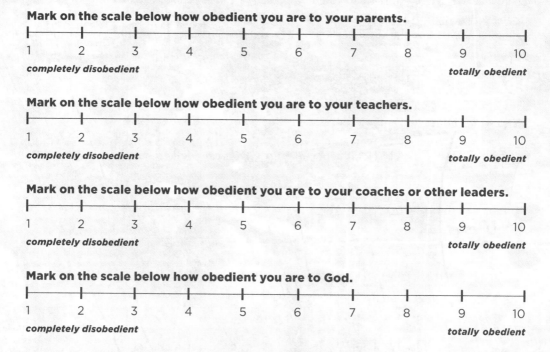

Mark on the scale below how obedient you are to your parents.

| 1 | 2 | 3 | 4 | 5 | 6 | 7 | 8 | 9 | 10 |

completely disobedient   *totally obedient*

Mark on the scale below how obedient you are to your teachers.

| 1 | 2 | 3 | 4 | 5 | 6 | 7 | 8 | 9 | 10 |

completely disobedient   *totally obedient*

Mark on the scale below how obedient you are to your coaches or other leaders.

| 1 | 2 | 3 | 4 | 5 | 6 | 7 | 8 | 9 | 10 |

completely disobedient   *totally obedient*

Mark on the scale below how obedient you are to God.

| 1 | 2 | 3 | 4 | 5 | 6 | 7 | 8 | 9 | 10 |

completely disobedient   *totally obedient*

- **Which authority figure in your life do you find most difficult to obey? Why?**

- **What keeps you from fully obeying God? Why?**

Invite a student to read aloud John 14:15.

- **What is the simple message in this passage? What does it have to do with evangelism? Explain.**

Admit that you realize students may be getting antsy about getting to the how-to of evangelism. But stress that Ed intentionally structured **My 8** this way, wanting to help them come to the conviction that they must share with others what they have experienced through Christ—out of desire to do so, not out of guilt.

In order for students to come to that conviction, Ed needed to lay down several foundational principles, namely that:

- *We were created for eternity and arrested by grace.*
- *We regard worship as the fuel for our service*
- *We are committed to sharing Jesus in the Holy Spirit's power regardless of the opposition we face.*

Emphasize that if we hadn't taken the time to deal with each of these principles and Ed had just given the students a quick-fix guide to evangelism, persecution would have silenced them. Now, because we have a deeper understanding of how, why, and with whose power we share our faith, we can be bolder than ever, filled with a great love for Jesus and the people who need to know Him. Emphasize to students that this love should motivate their obedience.

- **How would you explain the phrase, "It's not about your ability, but your availability"?**

State that God is not studying resumés to see if you're talented enough to carry His message to the world; He's just looking for surrendered, obedient hearts.

CLOSER LOOK

This section allows you and your students to dig deeper into the themes and topics Ed introduced in the video. Use the Scripture and information below to guide your discussion.

Invite a student to read aloud Acts 6:1-4.

- **What was the problem the early church was facing? What was the solution? Explain.**

- **What were the qualifications of the men to be chosen?**

Direct students' attention to page 49 in their student books and invite them to list the seven men the early church chose to serve. Instruct students to circle the second name on the list. Explain that Philip, along with Stephen and five other men, was selected to serve the church. *(Note: This is not the disciple named Philip.)*

- **What makes a person "full of the Spirit"? How would you describe that person?**

- **Can only certain Christians—like your pastor, student minister, or missionaries—be full of the Spirit? Why or why not?**

Explain that all believers have the same measure of the Holy Spirit within them because the Holy Spirit is not an "it" or a force. He is the third person of the Trinity, and His presence takes up residence within all those who are redeemed of God. Therefore, someone who is "full of the Spirit," as Philip was described, is willing to follow the Spirit (Gal. 5:25) rather than quench the Spirit's word (1 Thess. 5:19).

- **What does it mean to quench the Spirit?**

Explain that one of the ways we quench the Spirit is refusing to do what the Spirit tells us to do. A Spirit-filled believer responds to the prompting of the Lord with a resounding yes.

Call for a student to read Acts 8:5 aloud.

- **When the church was dispersed because of persecution, where did Philip go?**

- **Why could Philip have turned his nose up at this assignment?**

Provide deeper context to this passage by explaining that the Jews hated the Samaritans so much that they avoided even traveling through the region, even though that was the shortest route from Judea to Galilee. Stress that this hatred was founded on prejudice. The Assyrians had taken the Israelite nation captive Israel in 722 B.C. The Assyrians intermarried with the Jewish people, causing an intermingled race. The Samaritans, then, served as a constant and ever-present physical reminder of Israel's disobedience to God's command not to marry non-Jews. Raised as a Jew, Philip would have been familiar with this mind-set.

Explain that Jesus shattered this mind-set when He chose to pass through Samaria. During the journey, Jesus stopped at a well and shared living water with a Samaritan woman (John 4). Understanding that Jesus was the Messiah, the woman told the Samaritans about Him, forging a path to a spiritual awakening that was fully unleashed in Acts 8 when Philip traveled to Samaria.

Enlist a volunteer to read Acts 8:5-8. Challenge students to read and record what happened as a result of Philip faithfully proclaiming the gospel in Samaria. Direct them to use the space provided on page 50 of the student book. When students have completed the activity, invite a few volunteers to share their findings.

Point out that revival had broken out in Samaria and Philip had the opportunity to play an important part in the process. Explain that Philip didn't get to stay in Samaria very long, though, because God had a new assignment for him.

Read Acts 8:26 aloud. Challenge students to think about how they would explain Philip's new assignment in their own words and record it in the space provided on page 50 of the **My 8 Student Book.** Direct students to underline the phrase "desert road" in Acts 8:26.

- **What does this phrase help you to understand about Philip's assignment? Why?**

Remind students that Philip was enjoying great ministry success in Samaria, but then God instructed him to leave that for a desert road.

- **If you had been Philip, what would you have been thinking?**

- **How did Philip respond in Acts 8:27?**

Emphasize that Philip was completely obedient to God's call. Urge students not to overlook the six monumental words in Acts 8:27: "So he got up and went." This is the picture of a man whose heart was full of the Spirit. Philip lived out John 14:15, demonstrating pure obedience to the tender voice of God to leave what he considered to be the center of God's will and go to the desert.

Challenge students to think about what kinds of things you would (or wouldn't) expect to find in a desert. Allow time to discuss this, then point out that you definitely wouldn't expect to find water or people in the desert. Guide students to wonder and wrestle with if God's command made any sense (from a human standpoint).

- **How does the end of verse 27 help us understand why Philip was called to go to the desert road?**

Explain that Philip was going to have a divine collision with a significant person.

- **According to the Scripture, why would the Ethiopian man have been considered significant? And why was he on this road?**

Point out that the Ethiopian man was a court official and in charge of the treasury of an entire nation. He had come to Jerusalem to worship and was returning home. However, he could have been returning with disappointment in his heart. Because he was a eunuch, the Ethiopian official wouldn't have been allowed to enter the temple. So, he may have traveled hundreds of miles only to be rejected. Help students see that two worlds are about to collide, and one will be forever changed! Emphasize that when we submit to the leadership of the Holy Spirit, God will orchestrate divine appointments so we can share the hope we have in Jesus.

NEXT STEPS

Remind students that when they present themselves as fully available to God, He will be faithful to intersect their lives with people who need to know Him. They don't have to put on a great performance, just listen to the Spirit and choose to walk in God-consciousness, understanding that God is at work in every scene, every story, and every scenario.

Encourage students each day to . . .
* answer God's invitation to join Him in His work.
* pray that they would see the places and items on their schedules as opportunities to share their faith.
* notice how the people they meet, the places they go, and the priorities of their lives begin to look different.
* approach every situation, every conversation, every appointment, every errand, every destination with this question to God,with this question: *Whose life have You caused to intersect with mine so I can share about You?*
* be prepared for God to lead you down a proverbial desert road for a divine collision.

Review
Help students to consider what they've learned from this session. Challenge each student to jot down the three key truths they learned in this session on page 52 of their student books. Allow them time to work individually, then invite a few students to share their responses. Discuss these briefly.

My 8 List
Direct students to write in the five names that currently reside on their **My 8 Lists** and prayerfully ask God to help them be sensitive to each person's needs. Pray that God would continue to draw those people to Himself. Direct students to leave the sixth line on their list blank. The blank line will represent the person that God is going to strategically place in your life so he or she can hear the gospel. Pray that you would be aware of this divine collision and be obedient to share Christ with that person.

Scripture Memory
Group students into pairs and instruct them to review the previous My 8 memory verses with their partners. These verses include: Romans 1:16; Romans 3:10; Romans 3:23; Romans 5:8; and Romans 10:9. After the review, direct your students to add verse 10 to Romans 10:9 and work on memorizing them as a passage:
> *If you confess with your mouth, "Jesus is Lord," and believe in your heart that God raised Him from the dead, you will be saved. One believes with the heart, resulting in righteousness, and one confesses with the mouth, resulting in salvation.*

SESSION 7 **MY PRACTICAL**

Session Synopsis

During this session, you'll actually move to the how-to of evangelism. Students will look at the next part of Philip's encounter with the Ethiopian as a template for how a witnessing conversation might go. This session contains more material than previous sessions, so plan for extra time to discuss everything.

WATCH

Watch the Session 7 video (included in the leader kit). Guide students to follow along with the viewer guide on page 54 of the **My 8 Student Book.** *The answers are below.*

1. When our life is committed and yielded to the leadership of the Holy Spirit, we now know that God is actively at work in someone else's life creating this <u>DIVINE</u> <u>COLLISION</u>.

2. Two principles to remember:
    A. The Priority of <u>OBSERVATION</u>.
    B. The Power of a <u>QUESTION</u>.

3. There has to be that moment when the conversation transitions into <u>SPIRITUAL</u> things.

4. Three questions you want to ask:
    A. *In your personal opinion, what do you think it takes to go to <u>HEAVEN</u>?*
    B. *Do you mind if I tell you how the <u>BIBLE</u> answers that question?*
    C. *Would you like to give your <u>LIFE</u> to Jesus Christ?*

5. It's not your faith in a prayer that saves you. It's your faith in a <u>PERSON</u> that declares you as forgiven and a son or daughter of God.

6. Salvation is not a feeling, it's a <u>FACT</u>.

Briefly outline the key points of the video and allow time for discussion.

STARTING THOUGHTS

Lead students through this portion of the study, inviting group participation. Use the content after each question to enhance and direct the conversation.

Direct students to complete the following telemarketer activity (also on page 55 of the student book). Feel free to group students into pairs or small teams to complete this activity.

Imagine you're a telemarketer tasked with the job of "selling" the gospel.
  • **Outline your calling strategy, then jot down the opening remarks of your sales pitch.**

After a few minutes, call for students to present their calling strategies and the opening remarks of their sales pitches.

  • **How would you feel if that is how we were actually supposed to share the gospel with people?**

  • **Why do we have such a distaste for telemarketers?**

Allow students time to discuss, but be sure to explain that one of the reasons we dislike telemarketers is because we don't trust their sincerity. Talk about how telemarketers sound as if they really care about us, but the main concern of many telemarketers—and their employers—is the bottom line. They're just looking for the next sale.

Help students see that if we're not careful, in our sincere desire to share the gospel, we will actually start caring more about the bottom line of getting another person to "pray the prayer," instead of truly caring about the fact that this person needs Jesus. With this kind of attitude, our unsaved friends will become projects to complete, rather than people to love.

  • **What does it mean to treat someone like a project?**

  • **What happens when we treat people in need as projects?**

Urge students to care more about the people, rather than the process. Remind students that every person matters, and that we are to see them as God sees them. We don't overlook the person in our hope for a conversion. We don't long for someone to be saved so that we can be recognized and applauded. Our obedience should not be motivated by the praise of people, but by a heart of love and gratitude for the grace God has extended to us. We should have a tender heart for those who have not experienced this life-changing salvation rather than a desire to receive praise.

This section allows you and your students to dig deeper into the themes and topics Ed introduced in the video. Use the Scripture and information below to guide your discussion.

Remind students of where we left off last session. Use the following information to explain how Philip and the Ethiopian found themselves together on the desert road.

- The early church experienced persecution which moved them out of Jerusalem into the world.
- Philip was led by the Holy Spirit to Samaria where he shared the gospel and a great work of God broke out.
- In the middle of the revival, he was given a new assignment by the Holy Spirit to go to a desert road where he met an Ethiopian man reading from the prophet Isaiah.

Point out that although great things were taking place in Samaria, Philip was obedient to the Holy Spirit's call and left to go to a desert road. He didn't know why or what God had in store, but he went obediently. It soon became apparent that he was on the desert road to meet an Ethiopian eunuch, a high official of the queen who was on his way home from Jerusalem, where he had gone to worship. Guide students to see from Scripture that the Spirit prompted Philip to talk to the Ethiopian official. So, Philip ran up to the chariot. Explain that in this encounter, we really get to see the practical nature of the **My 8** evangelism strategy.

Enlist a volunteer to read Acts 8:26-31 aloud.

- **What's the first thing Philip did when he ran up to the chariot?**

Allow a few students to respond, then, point out that the first thing Philip did was listen. Explain that Acts 8:30 clearly states that Philip heard the Ethiopian reading Scripture. Stress that the fact that Philip listened before speaking helps us to understand that divine encounters are about more than us divulging a lot of information. They're about paying attention and really listening to the person God has placed in our path. It is about us seeking to be invited into a conversation that goes beyond the surface to a deeper level.

Share with students two important elements found in the divine-encounter conversation: **the priority of observation** and **the power of a question.**

THE PRIORITY OF OBSERVATION

Explain that students need to:

- Take notice of everything around them that could possibly be leveraged in order to create conversation with someone.

- Look for opportunities to transition from a cordial greeting to a conversation of shared interest.
- Emphasize how important it is for your students to listen closely to the person's name and remember it, especially if this is the first time they have met.

Direct students to look also for the following, which can help them move the conversation toward spiritual things:

1. A Point of Interest:
Explain that this means you find common ground with the person you're trying to witness to. Direct a student to read aloud John 4:3-7.

- **How did Jesus find common ground with this woman?**

Point out that His first words to her weren't about her sin or how He could save her. His first words were, "Can I have a drink?" They were at a well; she had come to draw water; and He was thirsty. Asking for a drink was common ground.

Challenge students to work together in pairs or small teams to come up with a modern-day example. Direct them to jot down their thoughts in the space provided on page 58 of the **My 8 Student Book.** Discuss their responses.

- **How does this point apply if you already have a relationship with someone?**

Explain that with a friend, your students won't have to search for common ground; they already have it. Guide the students to think about the things they have in common with friends that could lead to a conversation about spiritual things. Help students to understand that they just need to be aware of how the Holy Spirit might be leading a casual conversation into a deeper one.

2. A Passion of Identity
Encourage students to take note of the things a person is passionate about—a sports team, hobby, or interest—and ask them about those things. Once again, direct students to work together to create a modern-day example of this concept. Instruct them to use the space on page 58 of their student books to outline their ideas. Allow time for a brief discussion.

3. A Problem of Insight
Challenge students to be aware of the things in peoples' live that could be a source of pain, contention, or conflict.

- **What are some things happening in your friends' lives that fit this description?**

Strongly emphasize to students once again that people aren't projects. In these situations, you must sincerely love and care for people. Approach them with a heart to minister, knowing that as you do, a door might open for you to share the gospel.

Remind students of the other key element in a divine-encounter conversation, the power of a question. Use the information below to guide your discussion of that concept.

THE POWER OF A QUESTION

Call for a student to read aloud Acts 8:30 one more time.

- **What was Philip's question to the Ethiopian?**

Point out that Philip posed an important question to the Ethiopian official: "Do you understand what you're reading?" Philip wasn't just looking for a simple yes or no answer. This question allowed him to transition from mere conversation to a conversation with eternal consequences.

Point out that a simple diagnostic question is essential in moving a conversation from surface-level issues to eventually sharing Jesus. It gives you the opportunity to move the conversation deeper without being intrusive. Direct students' attention to page 59 in their student books and point out the examples of diagnostic questions used by other evangelism-training methods, such as:
- *Have you ever thought about spiritual things?* (Four Spiritual Laws)
- *If you were to die tonight, would you go to heaven?* (Evangelism Explosion)
- *In your personal opinion, what do you think it takes for a person to go to heaven?* (FAITH Evangelism Training)

- **What might be another good diagnostic question?**

Admit that it might seem a bit awkward to just jump from talking about football or skating to a diagnostic question. However, encourage students admit the awkwardness and ask permission with a question like *I know this may seem a little crazy, but do you mind if I ask you something personal?*

- **Why is it important to ask permission? Explain.**

Point out that one of Ed's favorite diagnostic questions is the one from FAITH evangelism training: *In your personal opinion, what do you think it takes for a person to go to heaven?*

- **Why is this a good question? Explain.**

Explain that the question isn't threatening, and it allows the person to share his or her opinion, which most people like to do. The key is listening closely to the person's answer.

- **What are some answers you think you might hear when you ask this question?**

Help students to understand that if the person responds with anything other than placing his or her faith and trust in the finished work of Jesus, then you must assume that he or she has never been born again. Stress that we must always be careful about assessing someone's salvation. However, when people are quick to base the hope of their salvation on something they have done rather than on what Jesus has done, it's highly possible they have never truly experienced the grace of Christ.

Explain that if students are talking to someone and it seems clear that they don't have a relationship with Jesus, it's time to take the next step in the conversation. Encourage your students to ask something like: *Would it be OK if I shared how the Bible answered that question?* Explain that this question allows students to speak with authority that is more trustworthy than their own.

- **How does doing so make God the expert on salvation, rather than you?**

Allow time for discussion, emphasizing that by explaining what the Bible says, students aren't just giving their personal opinions, but answering from the authority of the Bible.

Explain that at this point in a conversation about spiritual things with someone, that person may not want to go any further with the conversation. Stress that if that's the case, we shouldn't don't force the topic. Instead, encourage your students to be gracious and challenge them to extend an open invitation to the person to talk further at any time.

- **What could be the consequences of pushing or forcing this conversation?**

This question could lead to a lot of discussion. Guide the conversation by explaining that this may be the first of many conversations that might result in the person's salvation. We don't want to push the topic and ruin the chance to share the gospel at another time, nor do we want to do or say anything that would make the person unreceptive to another believer's witness. Remind students also that we're not called to get results. Explain that life transformation is God's work and our responsibility as believers is to be obedient.

Group students into pairs and challenge them to practice what they've learned so far in this session. Direct them to talk together, taking turns moving the conversation from common ground to asking for permission to share their faith.

Instruct students to read Acts 8:30-35 silently, then direct them to summarize the verses in the space provided on page 60 in the student book. Point out that the context of this passage shows that the Ethiopian was reading from the scroll of Isaiah about the suffering servant (Isa. 53). The Ethiopian had little knowledge of the Scriptures, so he asked Philip if the prophet was speaking of himself or someone else. In asking that question, the Ethiopian official threw the door wide open for Philip to tell him about Jesus.

Stress that if your students are given such an opportunity, they must tell the person about Jesus. Explain that this is where the verses they've been memorizing throughout the **My 8** study come into play. Emphasize that knowing these verses and references by memory will allow students to explain the gospel clearly, whether or not they have a Bible handy.

To help students understand how a conversation like this might go, walk through the following example, provided on page 61 in the student book:

> *Do you mind if I share with you how the Bible answers the question of how a person goes to heaven?* (You receive an affirmative response.) *The Bible makes it quite clear that God is perfect and we are not. In Romans 3:10, the Bible states "there is none righteous, no not one." This means that none of us is not able to measure up to the standard of perfection that God requires. As a matter of fact, Romans 3:23 reveals, "that all have sinned, and fall short of the glory of God." To fall short means that we miss the mark of holiness because of our sin. However, I have good news for you. God knew that we couldn't save ourselves or meet His standard of perfection, so He made a way possible. Romans 5:8 reveals His plan for salvation by helping us know that "But God proves His own love for us in that while we were still sinners, Christ died for us!" See, Christ had to die for our sins, so we can go to heaven, because Romans 6:23 makes it clear, "that the wages of sin is death, but the gift of God is eternal life." My sin and your sin deserved death, but Jesus died our death, to give us life, forgiveness, and eternal life. So, how do you receive this gift? Only by believing and receiving Jesus as your Savior. Romans 10:9 makes that quite clear, "because if you confess with your mouth that Jesus is Lord and believe in your heart that God raised him from the dead, you will be saved." This is a choice that you have to make. No one can make that decision for you.*

- **What did you learn about sharing your faith using Scripture from this example? Explain.**

- **What are some key points you learned about sharing your faith from this example?**

NEXT STEPS

Help students understand that there's not just one way to share the gospel. Stress that sharing your faith story in Christ has to be marked by your personality and fueled by your passion. Encourage the students to take the principles of this resource and make them their own.

Review

Guide students in a short review of the session, then challenge them to list a few things that stood out to them on page 62 in the student book. After a few minutes, invite a each student to share one thing they learned from this session.

My 8 List

Direct students to record the first six names on their **My 8 Lists.** Encourage students to find a partner and pray for each person on their lists, as well as opportunities to share the gospel with those people. After students have finished praying, invite a few volunteers to share a testimony of how they've seen God work in the life of someone on their list.

Call attention to the seventh blank on the **My 8 List** on page 62 of the student book. Challenge students to record the name of someone in their circle of influence who has similar passions or interests.

Scripture Memory

Encourage students to review all of the memory verses they've learned so far. Remind students that they're not just memorizing these verses to be able to recite them, but rather to use them in a conversation about the gospel, as shown on page 61 in the **My 8 Student Book.** This week, students should add Romans 10:13 to the list. Encourage them to work hard to memorize all these verses by next week:

- Romans 1:16
- Romans 3:10
- Romans 3:23
- Romans 5:8
- Romans 10:9-10
- Romans 10:13: *For everyone who calls on the name of the Lord will be saved.*

SESSION 8 **MY PRAYER**

Session Synopsis

In this session, you will show students how to finish the witnessing conversation, bringing someone to the point of a decision for Christ. Also, you will challenge students to not just move on to the next study, but to truly grasp the eternal impact of being an effective, lifelong witness for Christ.

WATCH

Watch the Session 8 video (included in the leader kit). Guide students to follow along with the viewer guide on page 64 of the **My 8 Student Book.** *The answers are below.*

1. When someone gives their life to Christ there is a celebration in heaven, and you have played a vital <u>ROLE</u> in that process.

2. The Ethiopian eunuch goes back to his position of influence—his position of prominence—and he takes the gospel of <u>JESUS CHRIST</u> with him.

3. The **My 8** movement is more than you just going through some <u>CURRICULUM</u>, checking off a box, and saying, "I did this."

4. You have no idea how your life can divinely <u>INTERSECT</u> with someone else, them coming to know Christ, and how far they'll carry the name of Jesus.

Discuss with students the key points of the video. Allow time for any questions.

STARTING THOUGHTS

Lead students through this portion of the study, inviting group participation. Use the content after each question to enhance and direct the conversation.

- **What are some of the biggest decisions you and your friends will be making in regard to your future in the next few days, weeks, months, or years?**

Direct attention to the space on page 65 of the student book and instruct students to work individually to list their ideas. After allowing them sufficient time to work, call for volunteers to share a few thoughts. Allow time for discussion, then point out that the greatest decision any of us will ever make is what we do with Jesus.

- **Have you dealt with that decision personally? Explain.**

This is an introspective question, designed to help students wrestle with their own standing before God. Challenge students to journal their thoughts on page 65 of the student book.

Allow students time to work, then explain that if they hesitated in writing their responses because they are unsure where they stand with Christ, they need to stop and consider what they've been studying the last few weeks. Take a moment to make sure the gospel message is clear. Explain that sinless Jesus took our sin upon Himself, becoming the perfect sacrifice to redeem us and reconcile us back to God. In His grace, God has extended the free gift of eternal life to us. In order to receive that gift, we must repent and place our faith in the finished work of Jesus on the cross.

At this point, students can complete one of two activities:
- Provide a moment for any student who has not made that decision to do so. Point to the provided space on page 65 of the student book to journal their prayer of repentance and faith. Encourage any student who just made that decision—or anyone who has further questions—to talk with you after the session.
- Direct those who have already made the decision to follow Christ to write about how they came to faith in Christ in the space provided on page 66 of the student book. If time permits, invite a few students to share their stories.

Share that it's now time for those of us who have accepted the invitation to follow Jesus to extend that invitation to others.

CLOSER LOOK

This section allows you and your students to dig deeper into the themes and topics Ed introduced in the video. Use the Scripture and information below to guide your discussion.

Point out that we concluded the previous session with two guiding principles: the Priority of Observation and the Power of a Question. Explain that both of these principles are reflected in Acts 8 and serve as key steps in leading someone to Jesus. In the last session, we looked at three distinct questions that propels you to the last question.

Challenge students to review Session 7 by filling in the blanks on page 66 in their student books. The answers are listed below.

1. Do you mind if I ask you a **PERSONAL** question?
2. In your personal **OPINION**, what does it take for a person to go to **HEAVEN**?
3. Would it be **OK** if I shared how the **THE** **BIBLE** answers that question?

Call for a student to read Acts 8:26-35 aloud. Briefly summarize the story for the students. Point out that when the Ethiopian expressed his confusion about the passage from Isaiah, Philip responded by using Scripture to "tell him the good news about Jesus."

Read Acts 8:36-38 aloud.

- **How did the Ethiopian official respond to the gospel? Explain.**

- **As they traveled by some water, the Ethiopian wanted to know what kept him from being baptized. How did Philip respond?**

- **What is the purpose of baptism? Explain.**

Some students may be unclear about the purpose of baptism. Take a few moments to explain that baptism doesn't supernaturally wash all our sins away. The blood of Jesus does that. However, baptism does testify to the heart transformation that Jesus has wrought in our lives. Baptism is a public statement of a personal decision to receive and follow Christ.

Direct attention to Acts 8:37 and emphasize that Philip made it very clear that all that was required of the man to become a Christian and experience believers' baptism was a heart decision made in faith. Instruct students to record the Ethiopian man's statement of faith found in Acts 8:37 on page 67 of the student book.

- **How is the Ethiopian man's statement a reflection of what Paul stated in Romans 10:9-10? Explain.**

Point out that Philip told the Ethiopian official that he must believe with "all" his heart to be saved. Explain that Jewish theology clearly taught that the epicenter of a person's soul was his or her heart. The heart was considered the seat of the emotions. Therefore, the heart had become a symbol for that place where a person's will and emotions collide. Knowing this context, guide your students to understand that this type of belief isn't just a mental assertion, but also involves an understanding of who Jesus really is (the Son of God), repentance (turning from sin), and turning to Jesus as Savior. Stress that it was this decision to identify with Christ wholeheartedly that transformed the Ethiopian.

Emphasize that as we choose to live out the **My 8** lifestyle, we must make sure that those we invite to give their lives to Christ understand that there is a moment in which they have to make a choice. To help students better understand this, direct their attention to the example of a witnessing conversation in Session 7. It's found on page 61 of the student book.

After students have had a chance to review, point out that we got to this point in the conversation:

> *Romans 10:9 makes that quite clear, "because if you confess with your mouth that Jesus is Lord and believe in your heart that God raised him from the dead, you will be saved." This is a choice that you have to make. No one can make that decision for you, but you.*

Help students to understand that if they're talking about their faith with someone and it gets to this point, it's time to ask a very important question: *Do you want to give your life to Jesus?*

Once again, stress that if the person declines, we should respond graciously, not rudely. But if the person answers affirmatively, guide him or her to express their repentance and faith in prayer. Explain to students that it is vital that we guide people to understand that it is not the act of praying that saves them, but rather their faith in the finished work of Christ that brings salvation and the gift of eternal life.

Help students understand that they can give the person the option to pray in his or her own words, expressing his or her desire to be saved, or to repeat the words after you. Once again, stress that it's not the words that save a person, but rather the attitude of their heart. Because this is true, either method is sufficient. To help students as they witness, point out the following sample prayer on page 68 of the student book.

> *Lord Jesus, I admit I am a sinner. I repent of my sin and place my faith in you, believing that you died for all my sin and shame. I ask you to rescue me from the penalty of my sin, forgive me, cleanse me, and help me to follow you all the days of my life, Amen.*

- **If someone makes a decision to follow Christ, what do you think would be the next step?**

Discuss students' responses, then encourage them that the next step is to celebrate with their new brother or sister in Christ! Instruct students to inform new believers that they have made the biggest decision of their lives. At this point, your students should strive to help people who have placed their faith in Jesus to understand that they've been made new in Christ. Challenge students to discuss the importance of discipleship and the assurance of salvation we have in Christ.

Also impress on students the importance of talking with the new believer about how they need to move forward from this decision. They need to:
- Share their decision with someone they know.
- Get involved in a local church where they can grow and serve.
- Follow their decision with baptism, making their decision to follow Christ public and symbolizing that they are part of the family of faith.
- Take intentional steps to grow in his or her faith, like reading the Bible and praying.
- Seek to be discipled by a more mature Christian.
(Students can read this list on page 69 of their student books.)

- **Why is it so important that you help new believers take these next steps? Explain.**

- **How can you be an encourager who comes alongside new Christians to help them move forward in their new life with Christ?**

Invite a student to read aloud Acts 8:39-40.

- **What happened to Philip after he baptized the Ethiopian man?**

Explain to students that someone coming to faith in Christ isn't the end of the story; it's the beginning! Point out that Scripture doesn't give us any specifics about what happened to the Ethiopian official, but history tells us that the first nation in Africa to receive the gospel was Ethiopia! It's safe to assume that Jesus transformed this man's life, and he took the gospel back home to his people and began sharing the good news with them.

Help students to see that God's story is bigger than them and bigger than this one moment. Close the **My 8** study with a challenge to student: to allow God to fill their **My 8 Lists** year after year with names of people who need Jesus. Invite students to form pairs and pray over each other, asking that God would allow them to lead the people on their **My 8 Lists** to Jesus. Pray that those people would come grow in their faith and, in turn, lead others to Jesus. Thank God that His story goes on and on.

NEXT STEPS

Explain to students that **My 8** is not intended to be a study that they just check off their list and move on to the next one. Instead, it's designed to motivate them to embrace and engage the wonder of evangelism for a lifetime. Help students to visualize the ripple effect of the **My 8** movement by sharing the following challenge from Ed:

> *"As you see the eight people on your list come to know Christ, continue to fill that list with other names. Perhaps you would also consider taking eight other believers through this study as a way to disciple and mentor them so that they, too, would understand the call and compulsion to share the gospel. Think about this: you lead eight people to know Jesus, and those eight people lead eight more into a relationship with Jesus, who in turn lead eight others to Christ. Amazing, huh? It can through the power of Christ in you as you walk in obedience to His call and purpose for your life."*

Review

Guide students to think about what they've learned in this session. Ask questions like: *What words or phrases stood out to you? How did God pierce your heart with His Word? How will what you've learned change how you live?* Challenge students to list their responses in the space provided on page 70 of the student book. Invite students to share a few responses.

To review the practical how-to tips Ed presented in this session, consider providing time for students to take turns practicing witnessing conversations with a partner.

My 8 List

Direct students to add the first seven names to their **My 8 Lists.** To complete the list, instruct students to record the name of someone they've met since starting this study. As a group, pray for opportunities for each student to get to know the person they listed and share the good news of Jesus with them.

Scripture Memory

If students didn't review their memory verses as they practiced their witnessing conversations, give them a chance to do so now. These verses include: Romans 1:16; Romans 3:10; Romans 3:23; Romans 5:8; Romans 10:9-10; and Romans 10:13.

This week, challenge students to commit Romans 8:38-39 to memory. Point out that this verse will not necessarily be used in leading someone to Jesus, but will be good to share with a new convert to help him or her understand the assurance of salvation.

For I am persuaded that not even death or life, angels or rulers, things present or things to come, hostile powers, height or depth, or any other created thing will have the power to separate us from the love of God that is in Christ Jesus our Lord. —Romans 8:38-39